JABEZ: A FRESH PERSPECTIVE FOR A NEW GENERATION

In *The Prayer of Jabez,* Bruce Wilkinson blessed millions by showing how necessary and right it is for us to pray for ourselves. I join those millions in thanking Dr. Wilkinson for those life-changing insights.

The Healing of Jabez revisits the same, now famous, Bible passage about Jabez to reveal a second pathway, one that leads each of us to healing for our wounds.

—John W. Mauck

THE
HEALING
OF JABEZ

THE
HEALING
OF JABEZ

How God Uses Pain to Bring Healing

JOHN W. MAUCK

credo
house publishers

DEDICATION

I dedicate this book to my healer.

ACKNOWLEDGMENTS

Thanks to Quin Sherrer, Jhan Moskowitz, Margie Zivin, Dirk Wierenga, Melissa Harman, Tom Ciesielka—and my law partners, Richard Baker, Andy Norman and Whit Brisky for encouragement and help.

1 Chronicles 4:9–10

Jabez was more honorable than his brothers. His mother had named him Jabez, saying, "I gave birth to him in pain." Jabez cried out to the God of Israel, "Oh, that you would bless me and enlarge my territory! Let your hand be with me, and keep me from harm so that I will be free from pain." And God granted his request. (New International Version)

CONTENTS

Men of Love
Men of Forgiveness
Men of Expressive Faith
Men of Confident Faith
Men Triumphant

1

THE POWER OF A NAME

Dear Reader:

Would you allow me to introduce you to my friend Jesus? Perhaps you have already met another mutual friend, the famous, or some would say notorious, Jabez. *Millions have met Jabez as a man of prayer but before he ever prayed, he hurt.* Pain did not stop Jabez from prayer—it moved him to cry out to God! Jabez found the great secret of transforming suffering into rejoicing, of changing defeat into victory. In our walk with Jabez, Jesus will join us. I cannot tell you at what point you will note his presence because he often whispers.

> *Now Jabez was more honorable than his brothers, and his mother called his name Jabez, saying, "Because I bore him in pain."* (1 Chronicles 4:9)

Have you ever considered how profoundly names shape us? When we say "Guts" or "Pride" or "Spite" is someone's "middle name," we mean their core, their pith is defined by that name. With Jabez, pain was his first name, his ever-constant companion. More than simply "pain" his mother actually named him "He will cause pain." This name had a power over his life.

In the Bible names often epitomize a person's life. Consider Jacob. His parents gave him the name "Deceiver." Sure enough, that was the story of his life. Yet his life was also a struggle to obtain the promised blessings of God. As a reward, God renamed Jacob "Israel," "He who wrestles with God." Another example is "Yeshua," a Hebrew name meaning, "Yahweh (God) saves." In English Yeshua is "Jesus." In all human societies, names bring self-identity, family identity and social identity. The more particular the name and the more specific its meaning, the more deeply that name shapes identity, sense of self. That is why nicknames or reputations can bless or wound. Have you known kids with labels such as "stinky," "brains" or "pimples"? How did those names change them?

Although Israel and Jesus were blessed by their names, the Bible has examples where names were a curse. Nabal was rich. Yet the Bible tells us his name meant "fool," (1 Samuel 25:25). Nabal was asked to help the man God had chosen to become king of Israel, David. David and his men needed food and Nabal had plenty. Yet Nabal spurned the advice of his wife and servants, he hoarded his food and possessions, he insulted David, and he acted the fool. He acted out his name and in folly, destroyed his life. Fearing the justice his own actions might bring him, Nabal died from a stroke.

Often a name can be a curse when given but can turn into a blessing. Whether a name remains a curse can depend on the response of the person bearing the name. Jabez was cursed at birth by being named "Pain," but he turned his curse to blessing. Not only does the Bible tell us the meaning of his name but also it says he got the name because his mother suffered pain in childbirth, possibly extraordinary pain. She blamed her son. She put the pain she suffered on her innocent child. However the source of her pain, the Bible tells us, was her maternal ancestor. Eve, through sin, brought a curse on women in childbirth:

And the Lord God said unto the woman, What is this that thou hast done? And the woman said, The serpent beguiled me, and I did eat. (Genesis 3:13 KJV) To the woman He said: … In pain you shall bring forth children; … (Genesis 3:16)

The mother of Jabez inherited this curse, this pain. Although it was not for her own sin she suffered, she did not need to pass this pain on to her son. She chose to do so. Focusing on her own suffering, she selfishly put suffering on the child she could and should have loved.

Have you been "named"? Not just our given names but the words and attitudes of those around us shape us. Have you been called "stupid" or "ugly" by classmates? Did your family label you "weak" or "incompetent"? Do the words "unmarried," "drop-out," "fatty" or "divorced" knife your heart? The hurt to Jabez cut as deep or deeper. Understanding how deeply he was wounded and understanding how we ourselves are wounded is the first step to receiving the same healing Jabez received.

PAIN FROM A MOTHER

Mothers, by nature, by God's design, nurture the child in their womb and the child to whom they give birth. A baby is helpless and fully dependent, both in body and spirit, especially on his or her mother. As toddlers we learn to give love as we experience the love others give us. And mothers are God's first way of loving us and teaching us to love. When Jabez first heard his name, he did not understand its meaning—he only came to know that the sound, "Jabez," meant him. He first accepted that identity without its meaning.

Most Americans have a name which has no apparent meaning in English especially to a child. When my mother called me John I learned to respond. Much later I came to understand it referred to a great uncle who had died a generation before my birth. But to Jabez, his name had immediate meaning in his own Hebrew tongue. Children feel pain—a scrape, an ache of hunger, a spanking, loneliness, and fear. First Jabez learned his name. Then one day he learned the meaning of his name and the little boy connected it with those feelings of pain. As the shame and confusion flushed through him, to whom would he turn? "Mommy, why am I called Jabez?" "Jabez, I named you Pain because when you were born you caused me great suffering."

May we assume the small child Jabez craved love and affection from his mother? All children do. May we assume he wanted to love his mother? What child doesn't? Yet this child learned at a tender age, that his mother considered him such a source of pain to her that she would remind him of it whenever he was called to dinner, awakened in the morning or even potty-trained. In angry moods, her call of "Jabez" would have accused him.

Jesus talked about how most mothers deal with the pain of childbirth:

A woman giving birth to a child has pain because her time has come; but when her baby is born she forgets the anguish because of her joy that a child is born into the world. (John 16:21 NIV)

But not so for the mother of Jabez. She remembered. She could not let go or let others forget the pain she felt. She determined her son would carry her pain. Even in times of tenderness, if this mother did have them with her son, the "Jabez" would sting. Simple hopeful childish gestures, picking a wildflower for mother, brought risk of pain, for even his name spoken gently could be a rebuke. "Thank you, Jabez." Could he ever have escaped the guilt of wounding his mother? Certainly not as a child. Later, perhaps he might have understood that she hurt him because she herself was hurt.

Has your mother hurt you? Was her love conditional or not love at all? Do the wounds still sting? Childhood wounds are not your fault but to have them healed you must first allow yourself to feel them again. Take a moment, or a week, to write them out, to understand the source of pain as a first step to healing. A simple prayer can help: "Lord, by your gentle Spirit allow me to understand how my mother has hurt me."

WOUNDS FROM A MOTHER

1.

2.

3.

Understand also that a child's wounds can come from a father. Consider whether you have wounds from your father.

PAIN FROM A FATHER

In the Book of Chronicles, Jabez is mentioned in the midst of a genealogy of the men of the Jewish tribe of Judah. Although, some of the notable women are mentioned, mostly the genealogy is about the men. While many of the sons are omitted from the listing, rarely is a man mentioned without reference to this father. A man's father was part of his identity. Many male descendants of Judah, the father of the greatest of Israel's tribes, are listed in 1 Chronicles 2 through 4. Yet the father of Jabez is never named. Various Bible scholars guess that the father of Jabez was Koz, Aharel or Harum mentioned in 1 Chronicle 4:8, however in view of the care with which the genealogies are recorded, and most of all because no father is named, it is more probable that Jabez's father is deliberately omitted. (Likewise the brothers of Jabez, and his mother, though mentioned, are conspicuously unnamed.) Did Jabez receive pain from his father? Yes, Jabez was hurt because he either had:

1. a father who refused to acknowledge him, not being married to his mother (and perhaps contributing to her pain at childbirth); or

2. a father who was so disreputable (as his brothers may have been) that he was omitted from Israel's roles; or

3. a father who though present failed in the primary duty of a father: protection. When his wife sought to name his son Jabez, a thought concerning the shame to the child and a firm veto would have been the minimal duty of a protective father; or

4. a father who was absent because of death or other cause.

Although we do not know in which of these ways the father of Jabez brought pain to his son, certainly Jabez suffered pain from his father from at least one of these relationships. Possibly he suffered from a combination of several. How would Jabez have felt toward his father when as a child he first realized that he had allowed him to be named Pain and throughout life called him Pain? If his father was absent, how would Jabez have felt growing up in what we call today "a single parent household"?

My own father, William Mauck, lost his father through divorce at the age of one and death shortly thereafter. He never knew his dad. Occasionally my dad told me of the pain of not having his own dad to play with him, teach him or watch him achieve. He wanted to be loved and wanted a father he could return love to. Like a valentine that could never be delivered, he carried this emptiness throughout his life. It may have contributed to many of his failures and disappointments. Certainly his expressed anger toward God, as a God who would allow a little boy to suffer so, hindered him from accepting God's saving love, until a year before his death, about twenty-five years ago.

Jesus experienced another pain Jabez may have felt: the pain of men calling his birth illegitimate, calling him a bastard.

> *Then they said to Him, "Where is Your Father?" Jesus answered, "You know neither Me nor My Father. If you had known Me, you would have known My Father also." (John 8:19) … They answered and said to Him, "Abraham is our father." Jesus said to them, "If you were Abraham's children, you would do the works of Abraham. But now you seek to kill Me, a Man who has told you the truth which I heard from God. Abraham did not do this. You do the deeds of your father." Then they said to Him, "We were not born of fornication; we have one Father—God." (John 8:39–41)*

Has your father wounded you or left you unprotected? Do you have an aching emptiness from an absent father, or one you never even knew? Has a divorce separated you from his care? Or have you felt cruel words from other kids who had a father when you did not? Take some time to think about the wounds you have from your dad. Write them down and ask the Lord to give you loving understanding of your father and to do so without bitterness.

WOUNDS FROM A FATHER

1.

2.

3.

While we reflect on how our parents have hurt us perhaps we should allow ourselves to revisit one other source of pain. If the wounds are not too tender, if the thought is not overwhelming, let us also consider how the other members of our family, our brothers and sisters have hurt us. Jabez had brothers who hurt him. If you are feeling overwhelmed, put this book aside for a while or, skip just ahead to the section on ***The Power and Heart of God to Heal***. Later come back for healing of the wounds from your siblings after you begin to receive healing from God in other areas.

Pain from Brothers and Sisters

"Now Jabez was more honorable than his brothers … " (1Chronicles 4:9). Most children tease and speak hurtful words to their sisters and brothers. Ever since Cain, the first son of Adam and Eve, murdered Abel, the second son, sibling rivalry has plagued humanity. Especially when one child appears more favored or more talented than his brother or sister, the rival sibling feels the pain of jealousy and often repays pain with ever more pain.

And in the process of time it came to pass that Cain brought an offering of the fruit of the ground to the Lord. Abel also brought of the firstborn of his flock and of their fat. And the Lord respected Abel and his offering, but He did not respect Cain and his offering. And Cain was very angry, and his countenance fell. (Genesis 4:3-5)

When God approved his brother Abel's proper offering but not his own, Cain conceived a murderous jealousy.

Later in the Book of Genesis, Jacob, whose name was changed to Israel, has twelve sons who become the fathers of the twelve tribes of Israel. Joseph was the son of Israel's favorite wife: the beginning of jealousy from his brothers. Then when Joseph received a prophetic dream that he would be honored above his brothers and when his father showed him special favor, the anger of his brothers caused them to sell him into slavery.

Now Israel loved Joseph more than all his children, because he was the son of his old age. Also he made him a tunic of many colors. But when his brothers saw that their father loved him more than all his brothers, they hated him and could not speak peaceably to him. Now Joseph had a dream, and he told it to his brothers; and they hated him even more. So he said to them, "Please hear this dream which I have dreamed: There we were, binding sheaves in the field. Then behold, my sheaf arose and also stood upright; and indeed your sheaves stood all around and bowed down to my sheaf." (Genesis 37:3–7)

Jabez, like Joseph, had more honor than his brothers. Would not these brothers have reminded him "you are mama's pain"? Would they not have used his name as a weapon in their competition and have been jealous of his more honorable nature?

Family wounds can cut most deeply. Surely Jabez knew the self-doubt, insecurity, inner reproach and perhaps even self-hatred resulting from a family which marked him as Jabez. On his journey to healing surely Jabez came to understand others, even his own family. He saw their wounds and no longer expected they would be his healers. We will see that he came to expect healing from another source.

Add the wounds from your sisters and brothers to the list of wounds from mother and father. Do not make the list for revenge but so that your wounds can all be brought before the Lord who heals.

WOUNDS FROM BROTHERS AND SISTERS

1.

2.

3.

Perhaps you have been as much a wounder as wounded. Have you abused, wounded or aborted your own child? Have you belittled your sister to make yourself seem bigger? If you know your need, there is hope for your healing both as wounded and wounder. Will you take the risky next step with me?

THE POWER AND HEART OF GOD TO HEAL

"And Jabez called on the God of Israel … " (1 Chronicles 4:10) … *for he who comes to God must believe that He is, and that He is a rewarder of those who diligently seek Him.* (Hebrews 11:6)

The God of the Bible, the God of Israel is a God who heals. "For I am the Lord who heals you" (Exodus 15:26). Literally, God reveals Himself by the Hebrew name *Yahweh Raphe*, the Lord who heals. Speak His Name. Trust His Name. *Yahweh Raphe*. Jabez believed when he prayed that God *could* heal and certainly dared to hope that God *would* heal. Do you believe in the power of God to heal? Do you think he wants to heal you? While sometimes we doubt the ability of God to heal, more often we acknowledge his healing ability, but question *his desire to heal us.* Jesus encountered such a man, a leper:

And it happened when He was in a certain city, that behold, a man who was full of leprosy saw Jesus; and he fell on his face and implored Him, saying, "Lord, if You are willing, You can make me clean." Then He put out His hand and touched him, saying, "I am willing; be cleansed." Im-

*mediately the leprosy left him. And He charged him to tell
no one, "But go and show yourself to the priest, and make
an offering for your cleansing, as a testimony to them, just
as Moses commanded." (Luke 5:12–14)*

Consider the Leper's "if." He knew God "could" heal
("you can make me clean"), but he doubted whether God
"would" ("*if* you are willing"). Did you know that a leper
had wounds that went deeper than his body? Except in
the most spiritually mature people, leprosy would bloody
and scar *the soul*. The leper was required to shout "Unclean! Unclean!" (Leviticus 13:45), wherever he or she
went. To any leper such self-devastating words were a
socially imposed cruelty, a life long torture. To the Jewish leper, raised to equate ritual cleanliness with holiness,
such words exclaimed "Rejected by God! Rejected by
God!" The emotional pain for most lepers was surely intense, numbing the spirit. From such agony we can well
understand that the leper who fell before Jesus and believed God *could* heal would still question whether God
wanted to heal him.

Jabez, by hearing the name which others called him
and by hearing the echo of what he called himself, endured a pounding of his spirit similar to that which the
leper suffered. But listen to, watch and feel how Jesus
responded to the leper's plea:

Then He put out His hand and touched him, saying, "I am willing; be cleansed." Immediately the leprosy left him. (Luke 5:13)

Jesus touched. This leper may not have felt the touch of another human, certainly not of a non-leper, for a long time. Jesus did not fear contamination. Rather, he knew his touch cleansed. Then, Jesus spoke. He spoke first his heart to heal, his love, "I am willing." Then he spoke to healing, "be cleansed."

Are you "unclean"? Perhaps your weight makes you think that wherever you go your appearance is shouting out "Rejected by God! Rejected by God!" (Leviticus 13:45). Maybe you carry around your skin color, skin condition, height, breast size, family background, lack of education, stutter, or the clothes you can afford as your leprosy—your shout of "Unclean!" "Rejected by God!"

Perhaps, your own actions, your sins, have put a foreboding of death in your spirit and you walk around feeling like everyone can see your inner ugliness. Have you put Jabez or leprosy on others? Have you aborted or abused a child, knifed your friend with words or rejected those who needed your love or approval? If these or similar wounds or sins afflict your soul, I have good news—Jabez and the leper can lead you to the God of Israel, *Yahweh Raphe*, the Lord who heals, the God who can heal and *wants to heal you*! That healing may come soon and suddenly or it may flow gradually from a deep and thorough remaking of your heart, mind and spirit by the Lord. To make it easier for you to experience God's healing, I want you to understand that the nature, the will, the heart, the very essence of God is to heal, to make whole, to make well, to save.

Do not be ashamed of your wounds, your grief, and your pain. Instead take them to God. He has given us bodies, which wondrously heal themselves, doctors, counselors and medicine which relieve pain and help us mend. He offers us prayer as a path to healing.

The cover of this book, *The Healer* by the Jesus People artist Janet Cameron, depicts the compassion of God. Take a moment to study it and allow the message of God's healing nature to settle in your heart.

> *"When the sun was setting, the people brought to Jesus all who had various kinds of sickness, and laying his hands on each one, he healed them."* Luke 4:40 (NIV)

The leper and Jabez both **cried out** to *Yahweh Raphe*, the Lord who heals. Neither merely asked. Both implored God. The leper fell with his face to the ground and Jabez cried out. They expressed their desperation to God. Both were healed. If you still doubt the heart of God to heal re-

read this section and Luke 5:12–14 until the power of Jesus' love dawns in your soul. Dawn may come in an hour or in weeks, but if you seek it the sun will rise. (Listening to and singing Beethoven's *Ode to Joy* couldn't hurt!) If you now understand your need for healing and the power and will of God to heal, you must now consider *choice* as the next step to your own healing.

2

THE TRIUMPH OF JABEZ

And Jabez called on the God of Israel saying, "Oh, that You would bless me indeed, and enlarge my territory, that Your hand would be with me, and that You would keep me from evil, that I may not cause pain!" So God granted him what he requested. (1 Chronicles 4:10)

CHARACTER

Did you know that God uses our personality traits to heal us? The triumph of Jabez came through strong character, dependence on God and right attitude. Can you see it in the Scripture? Let me explain. Pain did not bring healing to Jabez, it only brought choice: how to respond to pain. In the natural world, sunshine causes butter to melt and mud to harden. Its effect does not hang on the character of the sunshine but rather on the quality of the object put in the light. Likewise, the effect of pain depends upon the character of the person feeling the pain. However, unlike butter or mud which have fixed characteristics, people can choose.

We all know people from distressing and troubled backgrounds who have become paragons of honor and character. And who doesn't know someone who had a good family and was born with numerous advantages only to live a life of sloth while blaming others for his failures? Jabez prevailed over his pain or perhaps, we may say, he prevailed through it. The Bible shows us the character Jabez *chose* in reaction to his pain: honor, dependence on God and a redemptive heart toward his suffering.

The honor of Jabez was explicitly commended in 1 Chronicles, verse 9: "Jabez was more honorable ... ." When pain comes, the bitterness, which shadows our anger, often poisons our heart. We become vengeful to the source, or supposed source, of our pain. Often the anger/bitterness is at some level of our mind or spirit directed toward God. Other times we withdraw into a shell of self-pity. The "victim mentality" the world urges upon us grows from a warped view of how to handle pain: just blame others. Do you blame your family for who you are? Is a poor school system at fault for your miserable jobs? Was your husband the sole cause of your divorce? Has racism kept you from becoming the man you want to be?

Jabez could easily have let bitterness rule him, hating his mother, family, society, self and God—but he did not. Instead he chose honor—a commitment to seek, obey and live truth. This choice led him to Truth: the God of Israel.

Do you consider yourself a person of honor? If you do, then truth should be your middle name; truth in small things, truth in large things—seeking the truth of who the God of Israel is and the true path in life wherever it leads. If you are not willing, with all your heart, to find truth then do not deceive yourself about being "honorable," you are not yet. Do not expect healing on the deepest level. Wholeness will not knock on your door, until your heart welcomes truth.

However, if you want truth with all your being but do not know if the God of the Bible is God, the one true God of the universe, the only God among the "gods" of this age then here is an honest prayer that will help you find genuine honor: "God of the Bible, *Yahweh Raphe*, if you are real and the one true God then lead me to yourself. I will seek to know the truth about you and will sincerely receive and follow truth as you show it to me."

DEPENDENCE

Jabez's life depended on God. Not only does the Bible say he "called upon the God of Israel" (some translators say he "cried out") but consider that the Prayer of Jabez (the *actual* prayer not Bruce Wilkinson's book!) became so well known in his time and it was so remembered by the generations to come and so identified with him that the writer of Chronicles focuses his description of Jabez on just two things: his pain and his prayer.

An epitaph is an engraving on a tombstone, usually short—like "loving father," because although granite lasts, it edits strictly. In ways similar to an epitaph, the chronicler of Israel's tribes needed to describe Jabez succinctly because the genealogies were extensive and papyrus writing slow. The prayer itself reveals further his complete God-dependence in the intimate way Jabez speaks to Him: " ... that *You* would bless me ... that *Your hand* would be with me ... that *You* would keep from evil." In each of these facets of life, which can be seen as a summary of all aspects of life: 1) blessing; 2) being with God; 3) staying away from temptation; Jabez depends on God. Another way to describe dependence is "to have a need for others or someone else." We can come to healthy dependence by understanding that "independence" can sometimes be self-deception: a way to hide our pain.

Sometimes we fear dependence. We see it as weakness. We hesitate to trust. Bad experiences or betrayal cause us to feel dependence is weakness. While self-reliance is right and good in many situations, too often we want to "go it alone." The key is balance. Start with God, depend on Him. Talk with Him about this stuff. As you learn to live with God as your friend and teacher you will learn to balance dependence and self-reliance.

Jabez came to know that he needed God. He needed to depend on Him. Have you come to realize that true need? One path to that realization is choice.

DESIRE FOR HEALING

In addition to character and dependence on God Jabez *chose* healing: " … that You would keep me from evil, that I may not cause pain." Our English translations of the passage on Jabez contain a fascinating variation which can lead us along yet another path to healing. The New King James translators tell us that Jabez prayed "not to cause pain." A similar meaning comes from the King James, "keep me from evil." However, most other translations and the literal Hebrew tells us Jabez prayed "not to be in pain," (1 Chronicles 4:10). How do these different translations inform our understanding of the Bible's account of Jabez?

Simply put, the original text, not a translator's version is our light. Consequently, when a significant translation issue arises, we must avoid becoming doctrinaire or too authoritative based on an unclear or ambiguous version unless the lesson is confirmed elsewhere in the Bible. And, of course, if it is confirmed, our source of trust in the message of Scripture is not the disputed passage but the "confirming passage."

Happily, as we learn from the teaching of Messiah Jesus, the wisdom expressed in both variations of the Jabez prayer are confirmed by clear teachings elsewhere in the Bible:

It is good to want to avoid or be relieved from pain; and it is also proper, when pain comes, to seek to use it redemptively.

These harmonious attitudes are best expressed by Jesus in the Garden of Gethsemane as he prayed on the night before his crucifixion:

"Father, if it is Your will, take this cup away from Me, nevertheless not My will, but Yours, be done." (Luke 22: 42)

Jesus prayed to avoid pain, so did Jabez and so certainly should we. Everyone who is reading this book because it holds hope of healing, everyone who prays for others to be healed or sees a doctor affirms that avoidance or relief of pain is normally good.

When Jabez sought relief from the pain which his mother and life had hung upon him, he prayed according to the will of *Yahweh Raphe*. Yet many folks persist in seeing the will of God as the cause of illness. If you are such a person then I suggest that seeing a doctor or taking medicine is resisting God! Flirting with this book could bring an embarrassing blush of health. However,

I counsel you that God *wants you well* on your way to eternal life, so take your medicine, bless your doctor and keep praying!

Of course, the redemptive attitude toward pain—desiring not to cause pain to others despite the pain one feels—is also Godly. In the first chapter I spoke of my father's pain of not having a father. Despite the hollowing effect of this hurt on his life, Bill Mauck determined to be a good father *because* he had none. He largely succeeded.

Throughout human history exceptional people have sought to bring good out of evil. Though few, though wounded, they triumph. *Choosing* honorable character, dependence on God and a redemptive attitude toward pain is a step to healing. Have you chosen this path? Will you walk on it? Will you stay through darkness trusting light will dawn?

You must decide or you are not ready, you lack the will to be healed. God may heal you anyway, but it will be because of His undeserved love not because of your full cooperation. Jabez ranks among those special people who *choose* healing over and despite their wounds. His character, his dependence on God, and his redemptive attitude to pain were not only triumphant over his circumstances, *they produced his healing*.

By understanding and following the steps taken by Jabez to his triumph and to his healing, you too can overcome, you can be healed. Please allow me to lead you up the six healing steps of Jabez.

3

The Six Healing Steps of Jabez

"So God granted him what he requested." (1 Chronicles 4:10)

Jabez took six steps to healing. If you have been following his spiritual journey, if you have humbled your heart to follow God's way and not your own you are on the path to wholeness. You have completed three essential steps. Before we take the final three decisive steps let us review steps one, two and three to make sure we understand.

Step One: Acknowledge Your Need

Rather than deny the pain he suffered, Jabez acknowledged it in his prayer. Denial of our need often just buries pain, corroding our insides, creating a haunting specter in our hearts. But Jabez faced his pain, he named it.

Have you acknowledged the pains, the wounds of family, of friends and of enemies? Are you in touch with the pain life has brought you? Speaking to religious leaders who could only see the sin of others, not their own sins, Jesus said: "Those who are well have no need of a physician, but those who are sick" (Matthew 9:12). Do you have anxiety, sadness or fear?

Margie was full of worry. She loved her kids so much and wanted so badly for them to do well that she became fearful that if they did not study enough or were even late to school they would fail or at least not get into a good college. The result? Margie's fear and anxiety came out as anger—harsh hurtful words to those she loved. Perhaps Margie wanted to protect herself from her seeing, and thus feeling, her own hurt. But did her angry words help her kids? Usually not. Often they thought, "Mom's being mean." Sometimes they would snarl back or even be late on purpose to anger her further and be mean back to her! Sound familiar?

Ask God to help you see your own fears, needs, sadness or anxiety, and to face them. When you do it will help you avoid being hit by the boomerang of your own pain and also help you not hurt others.

Have you become so angry and hostile in defensiveness that you cannot or will not see your pain? Unless you put pride aside, look beyond your defensiveness and admit your need, you will be like those learned religious leaders, who could not be healed because they could not admit their need. You will be unable to take step one to healing.

If you want to be well, list your wounds, name them, face them. The truth may hurt for a while. Looking squarely at our own hurt, honestly seeing our own vulnerability takes strength. Rather than being a sign of weakness, acknowledging our own pain demands courage. Jabez faced his pain. Will you brave yours? If you will then you are ready for step two.

STEP TWO: KNOW GOD'S HEART

God not only has the power, but the heart and the desire to heal you. Faith, trust in God, is here required. If you have doubts about God's heart, hash them out with God by talking to him or write him a letter. Do not be afraid to call a friend who loves Jesus to ask questions or to join in prayer. Here are several Bible accounts of healing by God. Read them and you will better understand God's heart:

a. the healing of a leper named Naaman (II Kings 5:1–27);
b. the healing of a paralyzed man (Luke 5:17–26);
c. the healing of a man born blind (John 9:1–47);
d. the healing of a man crippled from birth (Acts 14:8–10).

When you have faith that God can heal and when you know, or fervently hope and are willing to believe, *he wants to heal you*, you have completed step two.

STEP THREE: CHOOSE

As Jabez did, determine to base your life on truth, be a person of honor, decide to depend on God fully and firmly resolve, with God's help to turn all pain in your life into good.

If you have taken steps one, two and three and want healing, now take the final three steps.

STEP FOUR: APPROACH

Jabez came to God with his wounds! He asked, he cried out. The leper came to Jesus despite fear of rejection. He too cried out. Both Jabez and the leper put everything aside to come to the Lord. Both had faith but on their way to faith they had hope, hope that God could change them, give them new life and fulfillment.

Sometimes we acknowledge our pain but still hang on to it. We even cherish our suffering as if it makes us more acceptable to God. Besides if we give our pain to God how can we remain victims? What will we whine about? Speak to God aloud, softly or loudly. Tell Him why you have come and what you want. Seek!

If you have approached God believing He hears you declaring your need and asking for help with deep sincerity, you have taken step four and are now at the point where you need to turn away from your sin. Proceed to step five.

STEP FIVE: RETHINK

When Jabez prayed that he not cause pain he turned away from sin. Knowing that we have sinned can be much more difficult than knowing we have been hurt. Most of us easily blame others but begrudge any thought or word that blames us. However, the Bible clearly teaches "all have sinned … ," (Romans 3:23). Seeing our self as a person who has sinned, requires us to rethink our responsibility for the hurt and failures within and around us.

Another word for thinking anew or rethinking is repentance—a change of mind, change of heart and change of action—a turning around. Repentance requires taking responsibility for *our* role in the human debacle and for our part in personal and family debacles. Surely people have hurt you. Just as surely, you have hurt others.

Jabez was not at fault for the name given him; however he became responsible, as he grew up, for how he reacted to all who continued to wound him. He was responsible for his actions and reactions. Out of his nobility of character, his honor, his surrender to God, and his commitment to truth, even the truth of his own wrongs to others, Jabez was able to turn from his sin. We all want the blessing of Jabez but hope to skip our personal responsibility to change.

Are you ready to rethink? To be healed of the specific wounds on your list, you must take this strong step. As to each wound, carefully think about and then honestly write out your share of responsibility.

Marianne had a mother who continually criticized her. Try as she might, nothing Marianne did would please mom. After she married and started her own family, she gave up. She said to herself, "Since mom hurts me continually I will ignore her—no more talks, phone calls or information about my children to their grandmother." Marianne may or may not have responsibility for her mother's criticism, but she needs to ask God to help her see if her response to the wounds from her mother has gone too far. Is she really loving and honoring her mother or is she returning pain for pain? She also needs to realize that her mother may never understand her own actions. Can she lower her expectations of mom?

Certainly at some point in his life Jabez hoped people would stop calling him "Pain." Maybe he asked, even begged, but the name stuck. Yet at some later point he stopped worrying about changing others. He let go. He moved on. I'm sure he at once felt much better. Marianne could benefit by not expecting so much from mom. Marianne may be frustrated if she focuses on changing mom, but if she focuses on changing herself she will move toward healing. Then she can love and honor her mother more freely and, ironically, with greater happiness and less stress both daughter and mother can change more easily.

This prayer sincerely spoken will help you see your own sin so you can know what to repent of. "Lord, show me how I have sinned in each place where I am wounded. Help me to see clearly, not blaming myself for the sin of others but not avoiding my own responsibility. Help me also to see how I can make amends wherever I have sinned."

God looks to our heart. After he murdered Uriah, his loyal supporter, the repentant King David also cried out:

The sacrifices of God are a broken spirit, A broken and a contrite heart—These O God, You will not despise. (Psalm 51:17)

If you do not feel you have wronged others or you are hiding behind that weak excuse "Nobody's perfect!" Stop! Wait. Pray.

On my journey of faith, I heard a preacher say "all have sinned." Those words offended me. I admitted, "surely Northern Irish terrorist bombers are evil but I am far from them!" A few weeks later my eyes were opened to see greed in some of my legal clients and then in lawyers with whom I practiced. I retreated to the solace that at least I and my friends were good. However, soon I was reminded, I believe by God's Holy Spirit, of when those friends had together woven a lie which hurt another friend. Okay, they were sinners—but I had not plotted with them. Surrounded, almost, by sinners—what a world! Then one day while shaving I looked into the mirror and thought a thought that left me lonely, "John, … you are married to a sinner." I realized my dear wife Rosemary was often selfish, ranking her wants ahead of mine, ignoring my orders! By now, dear reader, you may think that only you and I are sinless.

If you think that—think again! I came to see my sinfulness and that it ran deep. I realized that I would always bend my thought to excuse myself and blame others. I often judged others but never judged John. My values arose from what was good for me. Amazing grace could only come when I saw what a wretch I really was, the wickedness that dwelt within. If you think that you stand alone as a righteous person you are deceived. All have sinned.

Are you someone who hates being told you are a sinner? I mean do you feel abused, put down, beat up? When sin and your name are used in the same sentence do you feel angry and hurt? Is it like your dad saying "you are worthless"? If you said yes to any of these questions then listen carefully, read with an open heart and try to trust this advice. God loves you. So great is His love for you, comparison fails.

Speaking of God's love for his people the Hebrew prophet Isaiah wrote, "Can a mother forget the baby at her breast and have no compassion for the child of her womb? Though even she may forget yet I will not forget you. See I have inscribed you on the palms of my hands" (*see* Isaiah 49:15–16).

God so loved the world, which includes each of us, you and me, that He gave his own child, His beloved son Jesus that whoever would trust and give his life in dependence upon him would receive eternal life (*see* John 3:16). When Jesus freely went to the cross, when he took the nails in his wrists, you sinner and I sinner were given access to eternal life and Jesus engraved us not only on his palms but in his heart. Because of this awesome love, because God made us in His very own image (*see* Genesis 1:27), you can know yourself and see yourself as a person of infinite worth, a person valued by God.

Let me explain sinfulness in another way. We all do wrong, we all sin. Moreover we all persist in doing so. Have you broken a vow, betrayed a trust, failed to keep a resolution or acted selfishly? Everyone has. This is sin and being a sinner. You are not worse than others. Or better. All have sinned and fallen short of the glory of God. (*See* Romans 3:23).

So as a person created in God's image, you can take comfort in your worth. As a person for whom Jesus was willing to suffer you can rejoice in your value. But as sinners, if we want to live and think in truth, we must not only acknowledge wrong, destructive and hurtful actions, but also admit the woundedness within which causes us to want to continue in the way of sin.

Theologians call this woundedness the "sin nature" or the "flesh." You and I can call it that or use a mouthful of words: our natural desire to act contrary to what God wants. The Apostle Paul explained that there is nothing good about this impulse to sin which we all have. He points out its catastrophic effect on ourselves and others: "For I do not do the good I want, but instead the very evil I am against is what I do!" (*See* Romans 7:18–19).

Continue to pray and ask God to show you yourself *as He sees you*. Not a pretty sight! You may not be able to see your wretched true self at once, it may take a few weeks but if you seek this truth it will come to light. Do not skip this step but seek honestly—remember you have *chosen* honor. Let your commitment to honor allow you to see yourself honestly. More diligently than you have recorded the wounds from others, now record your own sins. You will move toward healing. Turn from those sins, decide to change, decide to ask forgiveness from God and others.

MY WOUNDS TO OTHERS

1.

2.

3.

Hint: Your list may extend beyond 3!

So far in this book we have been thinking about how we have been wounded, victims. Although we all have received wounds, we all have wounded—carelessly, deliberately, thoughtlessly. Jabez experienced God's full healing. We must ask his forgiveness for wounding those he has made and given us as companions in life. We can do so by admitting (out loud!) to God the wrong we have done, by setting our hearts to be healers not wounders, and by speaking or writing sincere apologies to those we have caused pain.

When you have truly acknowledged your hurt, approached and sought God by calling upon him, when you have admitted your sin and repented sincerely from within, step five, you are ready for step six—receiving your healing.

STEP SIX: RECEIVE/COOPERATE

The promises of God are received by faith, by trusting in Him to honor what he has spoken through His prophets. The Bible is insistent and consistent that God answers those who set their hearts on Him:

> *But without faith it is impossible to please Him, for he who comes to God must believe that He is, and that He is a rewarder of those who diligently seek Him.* (Hebrews 11:6; *see also* Deuteronomy 4:29, Jeremiah 29:13)

Jabez's prayer shows he trusted in God to change his life. It shows his determination to receive God's blessing:

And Jabez called on the God of Israel saying, "Oh, that You would bless me indeed, and enlarge my territory, that Your hand would be with me, and that You would keep me from evil, that I may not cause pain!" So God granted him what he requested. (1 Chronicles 4:10)

Although the healing and blessing came from God, *Jabez had to cooperate with the prayer in order for God to answer it.* Let me explain why.

Greg is praying for a promotion at work. He believes his creativity, his work ethic and his initiative qualify him for a more responsible job. He prays constantly for the new position but fails to submit his new ideas, won't help overloaded fellow workers, never works late and declines special projects which would improve his skills and standing in the eyes of upper management! Will God answer Greg's prayer? No! Greg might be promoted by fluke but I doubt that his promotion would result from prayer. Not until Greg changes his attitude and behavior, will promotion come through answered prayer.

God cannot answer such a prayer because it is only Greg's words which seek an answer. Greg's will is obvious: that he remain at the same level, be demoted or fired!

A prayer which goes against the will of the person offering it is no prayer at all because the words spoken and the intentions of the heart oppose each other. Such a prayer is "half-hearted," we might well say it is only "half-prayer" or "double-mindedness."

"So God granted him what he requested" (1 Chronicles 4:10). We know Jabez cooperated with God, we know his prayer was whole-hearted because God granted his request. Bruce Wilkinson, in the *Prayer of Jabez,* wisely advises the reader to pray the Jabez prayer daily. Does he think God won't answer unless we are repetitious? Of course not! Rather, repeated prayer helps us align our words, our mind, our heart and our will in one direction. Thus, prayerfully, we come to the point where we say what we want and we want what we say, the place where we say what we believe and we believe what we say, the time where we act on what we believe and we believe what we act on!

Are you *really* ready for healing? Do you want the *godsequences*—the repentance, the forgiveness, the changes in your life? If so then your prayer of faith, brings you healing from God now! Cooperate then with what God has done, confidently walking in the liberty God has for you.

Will your healing be apparent immediately? Often. But often it will appear gradually.

Consider that Jabez prayed for enlarged territory, to be kept from evil and not to cause pain. He was able to make these requests because he had drawn close to God in his heart. But none of these requests could be granted as a one-time event. Jabez had a lifetime prayer and lifetime answers! 1 Chronicles 2:55 even offers the possibility that Jabez eventually had a town named after him which became a center of learning!: "And the families of the scribes who dwelt at Jabez were the Tirathites, the Shimeathites, and the Suchathites."

The healing you have come to—pain removed from heart or body is a sign from God, a sign He loves you and has an even greater blessing for you! If you want deeper and eternal blessing, a peace which surpasses anything you can understand, then let Jabez now introduce you to Yeshua, Yahweh who heals, Jesus.

4

JESUS, JABEZ AND HEALING

Jabez triumphed through his pain. In response to his commitment to God Jabez was healed. God created us to be healed, sometimes through the processes in our bodies, sometimes through medicine and care givers, sometimes through prayer. Wholeness came to Jabez in his heart, wholeness from the wounds of a name, from wounds of words, family and friends. He chose to live a life of Godly prosperity, healed, forgiving and free from the curse.

The healing of Jabez, and indeed all healing, are signs that point to the Healer.

And [God] said, "If you diligently heed the voice of the Lord your God and do what is right in His sight, give ear to His commandments and keep all His statutes, I will put none of the diseases on you which I have brought on the Egyptians. For I am the Lord who heals you." (Exodus 15:26)

As you realize and experience your healing, open your heart to meet the Healer. Is that Jesus? At the beginning of his ministry, Jesus claimed to fulfill words written by the prophet Isaiah 700 years earlier. Consider the power and depth of God's love sent down:

The Spirit of the Lord is upon me, because He has anointed me to preach the gospel to the poor. He has sent me to heal the brokenhearted. To preach deliverance to the captives and recovery of sight to the blind, To set at liberty those who are oppressed. To preach the acceptable year of the Lord. (Luke 4:18–19; quoting Isaiah 61:1–2)

"The Spirit of the Lord" which was and is upon Jesus heals at every level, deeply, completely! Jesus raised the dead, cleansed lepers, gave sight to the blind, restored prostitutes, and even made friends with tax collectors, men despised by their own nation. Because Jesus is the ultimate healer, the healings, miracles and the people given as examples in the Hebrew Scriptures, the writings of Messianic promise, contain signs pointing to how God works, to what the heart of God the Father is. Thus when the Messiah, the Christ, would appear he could be recognized as the true and fullest revelation of God to humanity. He would not be seen as an abstract distant God, a "divine idea," but rather all people would be able to encounter him in the midst of human history, through the history of Israel, the people God had selected for this privilege and in their own lives. Jesus was God's fulfillment of His promise to restore the people He had created.

Certainly Jabez was familiar with pain and healing. And anyone with even a simple knowledge of Jesus knows that he too was familiar with both. Yet on some level most of humanity experiences both healing and pain. Do the similarities between Jabez and Jesus run deeper?

Consider that the Hebrew Bible is suffused with the hope of a Messiah who would rescue and rule over His people. Every book of the Bible in some way speaks of Him. Sometimes as I read those scriptures I see His footprints on every page and feel His gentle presence as He walks beside me. Have you heard his whispers? If indeed the Hebrew Scriptures point to Jesus as the Messiah, then because the story of Jabez is told amidst those scriptures, can we look more closely at Jabez, his pain and his healing to find significant similarities to Jesus: signs of the Messiah?

5

JABEZ POINTS TO JESUS

MEN OF JUDAH

The parallels between Jabez and Jesus are profound and several. In fact, so striking are the similarities that I believe the man Jabez foreshadows the Messiah. Jabez points to Jesus. Although no father is named for Jabez, his appearance amidst the genealogies of the descendents of Judah (great grandson of Abraham) makes clear that he, too, is of that Messianic tribe. As early as the Book of Genesis, where Jacob blesses his sons, the Bible identifies Judah as the tribe into which Messiah would be born:

> *The scepter will not depart from Judah, nor the ruler's staff from between his feet until He comes to whom it belongs,* … (Genesis 49:10 NIV)

Jesus was, of course, from Judah: "For it is evident that our Lord arose from Judah, …" (Hebrews 7:14. *See also* Matthew 1:2–3 and Luke 3:33). The Apostle John describes Jesus as "the Lion of the tribe of Judah, the Root of David" (Revelation 5:5). If he were not from that special tribe he could not have been the Messiah, but he was. Thus the first similarity between Jabez and Jesus is that both are from Judah, the same family within Israel. Would you like to know other connections?

SOURCE OF PAIN

Both Jabez and Jesus were marked as infants as a source of pain to their mothers. With Jabez we are told that he caused this pain at his birth. According to Jewish custom (*see* Luke 1:59 and 2:21), Jabez was named on his eighth day. On the day of his circumcision his mother named him "He will cause pain." Jesus was a little over a month old (*see* Luke 2:21 and Leviticus 12:8) when his parents took him to the temple. At the temple Simeon, whom Luke describes as righteous, devout and waiting for the consolation of Israel prophesied to Mary concerning the ministry of her son, "And a sword will pierce your own soul too" (Luke 2:21–35. NIV) The Bible tells us both men brought pain to their mothers.

Perhaps Jabez continued to pain his mother or caused pain to others such as his brothers. With Jesus, however, we know that he did and ever does produce intense pain, grief and sorrow. So profound is the pain he produces that we must pause to comprehend its scope and then consider how a hurter can be a healer.

Simeon foretells that Jesus will cause pain to Mary only after he prophesies: "Behold, this child is destined for the fall and rising of many in Israel, and for a sign which will be spoken against (yes, a sword will pierce through your own soul also)" (Luke 2:34–35). Simeon foretold that Jesus would not only wound his mother but many in Israel. Jesus was more specific:

> *"Do you suppose that I came to give peace on earth? I tell you, not at all, but rather division. For from now on five in one house will be divided: three against two, and two against three. Father will be divided against son and son against father, mother against daughter and daughter against mother, mother-in-law against her daughter-in-law and daughter-in-law against her mother-in-law."* (Luke 12:51–53)

We need only look around us to see the pain experienced by those who set their hearts to follow Jesus: loss of friends, ridicule and even persecution. In the early '70s when one of my brothers who was then in his early twenties embraced Christ, I purposely campaigned to exterminate this faith using ridicule, anger, the promise of acceptance if he rejected Jesus and the prospect of rejection if he persisted. Since I have come to know Jesus myself, I have experienced not only the pain of rejection from many I care for but also grief, almost to the edge of despair over the hurts I have caused others and God. Jesus taught: "And he who does not take his cross and follow Me is not worthy of Me" (Matthew 10:38).

If someone claims to serve Jesus and does not experience resulting pain, she should question whether she is on his path. However our understanding that Jesus wounds may confuse us. If Jesus is a giver of pain, how can he be a healer? Is the man many call the Great Physician really a cosmic sadist?

To understand how one can cause pain in the service of healing we must consider that pain can be a blessing. Dr. Paul Brand, in his inspiring memoir, *The Gift of Pain*, written with Phillip Yancey, recounts his journey of discovery and understanding into the wonders of the nervous system. Seriously introduced to the horrors of pain as a British medical student treating wounded soldiers in World War II, Brand saw pain as the enemy. Later as a missionary doctor and leprosy researcher in India, he gradually changes his understanding until he comes to see pain as an ally in healing.

Lepers experience nerve destruction which prevents them from feeling pain, particularly in their extremities—hands, feet, nose, and eyes. However, Dr. Brand learned that the disfigurement or blindness which lepers suffered was not a direct result of the disease. Rather, because a leper cannot feel pain, he will unknowingly incur injury: a blister, or bruise. Because he does not notice, because no pain from the injury nags him, the small wound festers, infections grow deeper. Not only tissue but bones are affected.

At one time an estimated one-third of all blindness in the world resulted from the inability of lepers to sense dust or objects in the eye and blink reflexively. Brand and his patients eventually understood that lack of pain had horrible consequences, but the presence of pain could be a gift.

As I write these words, I have been sitting next to a woman in great pain. My mother, Nancy, had open-heart surgery yesterday. As she regains consciousness emerging from the haze of numbing drugs, she speaks of the ebb and flow of pain in her chest. She chose surgery knowing the pain which awaited. Yet the prospect of life with more vigor allowed her to brave the knife. Was not the doctor's cut kind? Pain seen through the eyes of a leper or a heart surgery patient is a blessing compared to the alternative. A short pain avoids a longer pain.

Can your pain lead you to wholeness? Jesus was frequently gentle with sinners. To a woman caught in adultery he said "Has no one condemned you? ... Neither do I condemn you; go and sin no more" (John 8:10–11). Yet Jesus also told his disciples "He who has seen Me has seen the Father" (John 14:9). This God, the creator whom followers of Jesus call "Father," has created a world which is full of pain. Is God cruel? Is He morally unfit to govern the universe? No! Consider that words which may wound deeply one person may, when spoken to another, be the painful truth, the message which can liberate and heal.

Paul wrote of the effects of hurtful truth communicated in love "For godly sorrow produces repentance leading to salvation, not to be regretted; but the sorrow of the world produces death" (2 Corinthians 7:10). Are you tired of the temporary relief of pain, the quick fix, the vodka of denial, which leaves many regrets? Then understand that the pain you feel might be God's road marker to your deeper healing. The pain which Jabez caused, in a symbolic sense, and the pain which Jesus causes, in a real sense can direct our paths to a healing without regret, a healing the Bible calls salvation.

MEN OF SORROWS

The promised Messiah is described by the prophet Isaiah in verses 52:13 to 53:12. In 53:3 Isaiah writes:

"He is despised and rejected by men, A Man of sorrows and acquainted with grief." (Isaiah 53:3))

Both sorrow and grief brought pain to Messiah Jesus. Jabez suffered from his name, Pain, and separation from his brothers.

Yet there may be an ever more direct connection between Isaiah 53 and the Jabez passage in 1 Chronicles. Jabez lived before Isaiah wrote. However, the writer of Chronicles, because he lived and compiled Chronicles *after* Isaiah, almost surely knew the messianic prophecies of Isaiah. Thus the unusual appearance of Jabez and the details about him, suggest the compiler interrupted his recording of family lines to speak of a man who had certain messiah-like traits, a man who resembled Isaiah's powerful man of sorrows. While we can only wonder whether the inclusion of the story of Jabez was a deliberate echo of Isaiah's man of sorrows, the similarities of both men leaves that deliberate connection as an open and intriguing possibility.

Whether or not the Bible records the life of Jabez in light of Isaiah 53, Jesus of Nazareth, who fulfilled Isaiah 53, surely experienced profound pain on every level. Physically, the scourging and the crucifixion he suffered were the greatest infliction of torture which evil humanity could devise. The wounds to his spirit pierced as deeply as the nails in his palms:

The sorrow of rejection by his brothers:

O Jerusalem, Jerusalem, the one who kills the prophets and stones those who are sent to her! How often I wanted to gather your children together, as a hen gathers her chicks under her wings, but you were not willing! (Matthew 23:37); and

He came to His own, and His own did not receive Him. (John 1:11)

The sorrow of loneliness, and emotional abandonment by his friends on the night of his crucifixion:

Then He came to the disciples and found them sleeping, and said to Peter, "What! Could you not watch with Me one hour?" (Matthew 26:40);

And the agony of the sins of others visited upon him:

He went a little farther and fell on His face, and prayed, saying, "O My Father, if it is possible, let this cup pass from Me; nevertheless, not as I will, but as You will. (Matthew 26:39)

Jesus felt the depth of emotional pain on every level.

Dear Reader, in your pain receive comfort by understanding that Jesus can sympathize because he has been in deep pain himself.

Jabez knew the pain of rejection, Jesus experienced that pain and other agonies on many levels. Yet both found in prayer the same solace and a source of strength.

MEN OF PRAYER

Both Jesus and Jabez are noted for their fervent prayer to the God of Israel:

And Jabez called on the God of Israel saying, "Oh, that You would bless me indeed, ... that your hand would be with me ... " (1 Chronicles 4:10)

[Jesus] who, in the days of His flesh, when He had offered up prayers and supplications, with vehement cries and tears to Him who was able to save Him from death, ... (Hebrews 5:7)

And the prayers of Jesus and Jabez both had an emphasis on staying out of temptation:

And Jabez called on the God of Israel saying ...that you would keep me from evil. (1 Chronicles 4:10)

Now it came to pass, as He was praying in a certain place, when He ceased, that one of his disciples said to Him, "Lord teach us to pray …" So He said to them when you pray say: "… and do not lead us into temptation but deliver us from the evil one." (Luke 11:1-4)

As both men hungered to know God and have God with them to satisfy that hunger, they were rewarded with God's presence, guidance and companionship. Their *hunger* drew the presence, the Spirit, the power of God into their lives.

HATERS OF PAIN

Both Jabez and Jesus rejected and hoped to avoid pain. Of course, it makes sense that those bringing healing pain, reject pain in other contexts.

Matthew, a disciple of Jesus, was an eyewitness to Jesus' agony the night before his death. He tells us Jesus prayed three times to be spared from crucifixion (*see* Matthew 26:39–44). Certainly Jesus knew the pain that awaited him and was imploring God for some way to avoid it.

Continue with me as we revisit the fascinating account of Jabez to see how he wanted to avoid pain. As we have thought about Jabez and his relation to pain, we have used the translation in New King James Version "And Jabez called on the God of Israel saying, 'Oh, that You would bless me indeed, and enlarge my territory, that Your hand would be with me, and that You would keep me from evil, that I may not cause pain!' So God granted him what he requested" (1 Chronicles 4:10). This translation (and to some extent the King James translation) tell us that Jabez did not want to cause pain, to cause evil. The translators may have considered the original Hebrew name Jabez in verse 9 "He will cause pain" to be part one of a word play which influences the meaning of part two, in verse 10 phrase " that I may not cause pain."

However we also considered that the literal Hebrew and most translations tell us that phrase in English should read "so that I will be free from pain" (New International Version). Jabez prayed to be relieved of pain. The context indicates that the pain he wanted freedom from was certainly that caused by his name and possibly that resulting from his family relationships. *Jabez's remedy for pain was "blessing" and "enlarged territory."*

Thus from the public and private pain from his name and his family relationships, Jabez sought healing by public success and, presumably, private satisfaction. This success, this balm to his wounds flows from the relationship Jabez has with God. Thus it can fairly be inferred that any material blessing Jabez received was both *from* God and to be used *for* God. Likewise when we pray for blessing and enlarged territory from God, we are wise to search our hearts, our motives, that we thus pray to serve God better and not to use Him because we love money. Money without God can be a curse.

Was Jabez right to want healing through success? Have you ever been to a high school reunion? Such affairs are inevitably attended by the high school ugly duckling who became the knockout business executive at age thirty or the coke-bottle-glasses nerd of sixteen who invented contact lenses at age thirty-five. However, at the reunion our ugly duckling has replaced her dirty feathers with black satin and our nerd now looks more like Denzel Washington than Gary Coleman. They have not come to the reunion to be dumped on again. Rather they long for healing: an admiring glance from someone who snubbed her twenty years ago or even, hope of hopes, an apology: "I should have recognized that you were a genius even in high school!"

Were or are you an ugly duckling or nerd? Is healing from success, from the esteem of others, Godly or just selfish? Rightly understood all healing is from God. And although we can surely seek healing for ourselves so as to bless others, most healing prayers are fundamentally self-ish. *When we ask God to heal us we are praying selfishly **and** we are praying according to God's will.* This type of selfish prayer is certainly proper—no one will be hurt by our healing. God loves us and wants us to be blessed.

So Jabez was right to seek healing through prayer—
prayer that he might be successful among his people. Our
ugly duckling and nerd are also right to seek healing in
the approval and affirmation of others. Yet such healing
also has a risk: what if we never get the approval we crave?
What if our classmates still treat us like dirt? What if,
despite our accomplishments our dad never says "I'm
proud of you!" Can we then never heal? Can wholeness
never be real?

The Bible and the actions of Jesus show us a more
excellent way, a surer, more lasting and complete path
to wholeness than being healed through the opinion of
others. Jabez points us this way also. The truest, most satisfying, surest and deepest healing through the opinion
of others comes from understanding, getting hold of and
grabbing into our hearts the opinion of God about us.
He is the great "other" whose approval we long for. God
created us in His image—in the first book of the Bible,
in the very first chapter we are told:

> *"So God created man in His own image: In the image of
> God He created him; male and female He created them."*
> (Genesis 1:27)

How wonderful to know that we are specially made
by God! Not like animals but in the very likeness of our

Creator! When we accept this truth by faith we can be healed of all the rejection by others. In God's eyes every "nerd" is a precious child, every "ugly duckling" a glory.

Yet, incredibly, the news about God's good opinion of us gets even better! God's esteem for us, His love, His approval, did not stop when He created us. He didn't just put us together and leave us like so many toys in the sand box. No, when He saw us helpless in the quicksand of sin, a plan of rescue immediately arose from the love in His heart for us. John, one of Jesus' first disciples explained this love in these words: "Because God so loved everyone He had created, He sent His own beloved son to die for their sins so that each person who would accept and trust this gift of God's love would not die, but instead would receive eternal life. (My loose paraphrase of John 3:16)

Dearest Reader, you personally are so loved by your Creator that He gave His son to die for you! Your self worth need not depend on the fickle opinion of classmates, family or friends. It can be anchored in the confident truth that you are as precious to God as His son Jesus. Will you accept this liberating healing truth?

If you accept, trust in and rely upon God's opinion of you, if you will allow your heart and mind and will to be changed so that God's opinion of you matters more than other people's opinion of you, then you will be free and healed. Like Jabez you will succeed in the plans God has for you. The angels of God will hail you like they hailed Gideon, "Mighty man/mighty woman of valor." (*see* Judges 6:12) (Although I cannot promise you'll see those messengers of God or hear aloud their heavenly acclaim!)

Most importantly you will become like Jesus in a special way. Jesus held firmly to the will of His heavenly Father, hearing His voice to the exclusion of the every opinion, ridicule of his enemies and discouragement of his friends. "Therefore Jesus answered and was saying to them, 'Truly, truly, I say to you, the Son can do nothing of Himself, unless it is something He sees the Father doing; for whatever the Father does, these things the Son also does in like manner'" (John 5:19 NASB).

Jesus, as we have also seen, like Jabez wanted to avoid pain. He did not seek pain, rejection by others or physical pain for its own sake. His prayer in the Gethsthemene Garden was "to let this cup [of suffering] pass." He was not a masochist. He did not enjoy pain yet he willingly endured the cross "for the joy [of seeing our salvation] that was set before him," (*see* Hebrews 12:1–2). Thus we can appropriately avoid pain but must only do so if God does not want us to experience it. Sometimes God has a higher purpose, a plan where small pain avoids bigger pain or brings better healing.

Doctors told Dick Hoyt his son, Rick, brain damaged at birth by umbilical cord strangulation, would be a "vegetable for the rest of his life." "There's nothing going on in his brain." Rick Reilly in *Sports Illustrated* tells how Dick responded:

"Tell him a joke," Dick countered. They did. Rick laughed. Turns out a lot was going on in his brain.

Rigged up with a computer that allowed him to control the cursor by touching a switch with the side of his head, Rick was finally able to communicate. First words? "Go Bruins!" And after a high school classmate was paralyzed in an accident and the school organized a charity run for him, Rick pecked out, "Dad, I want to do that."

Yeah, right. How was Dick, a self-described "porker" who never ran more than a mile at a time, going to push his son five miles? Still, he tried.

"Then it was me who was handicapped," Dick says. "I was sore for two weeks." …

Now they've done 212 triathlons, including four grueling 15–hour Ironmans in Hawaii …

"No question about it," Rick types. "My dad is the Father of the Century."

And Dick got something else out of all this too. Two years ago he had a mild heart attack during a race. Doctors found that one of his arteries was 95% clogged. "If you hadn't been in such great shape," one doctor told him, "you probably would've died 15 years ago."

So, in a way, Dick and Rick saved each other's life …

… [B]ut the thing he [Rick] really wants to give him is a gift he can never buy. "The thing I'd most like," Rick types, "is that my dad sit in the chair and I push him once."

It's worth a look at the video: Simply Google "Team Hoyt."

Hoyt father and son show us the same heart Jabez had. Who would want a son so handicapped? Which of us would choose to be born brain damaged and confined for life to a wheelchair? Yet Rick and Dick have turned their jabez into joy, blessing and health for themselves, overflowing in God's Spirit to us as we read, watch and listen.

Discipline within the community of believers in Jesus provides another good example of causing pain to bring healing. Jesus instructs us to deal gently, but decisively with a brother who sins against us:

> *"Moreover if your brother sins against you, go and tell him his fault between you and him alone. If he hears you, you have gained your brother. But if he will not hear, take with you one or two more, that 'by the mouth of two or three witnesses every word may be established.' And if he refuses to hear them, tell it to the church.*

But if he refuses even to hear the church, let him be to you like a heathen and a tax collector. Assuredly, I say to you, whatever you bind on earth will be bound in heaven, and whatever you loose on earth will be loosed in heaven. Again I say to you that if two of you agree on earth concerning anything that they ask, it will be done for them by My Father in heaven. For where two or three are gathered together in My name, I am there in the midst of them." (Matthew 18:15–20)

The intervention in the life of the one who has hurt us, described above, is designed to bring reconciliation between our brother, our self and God. Yet confrontation causes pain!

Once I confronted "Matt," a brother who was in a sinful sexual relationship. After I and several other friends counseled with him, he told us to kiss off. The Bible instructs us to break the relationship, I believe, in part for the benefit of the sinner, that he might come to his senses:

"I wrote to you in my epistle not to keep company with sexually immoral people. Yet I certainly did not mean with the sexually immoral people of this world, or with the covetous, or extortioners, or idolaters, since then you would need to go out of the world. But now I have written to you not to keep company with anyone named a brother, who is sexu-

ally immoral, or covetous, or an idolater, or a reviler, or a
drunkard, or an extortioner—not even to eat with such a
person. For what have I to do with judging those also who
are outside? Do you not judge those who are inside? But
those who are outside God judges. Therefore 'put away from
yourselves the evil person'. " (1 Corinthians 5:9–13)

So, I and Matt's other friends decided to stop associat-
ing with him. We felt then *our* pain, in losing a friend,
should be accepted and endured because of the faithful
love God wants us to have for each other.

We must not seek to avoid pain in all situations, but
in many cases must endure it as Jesus did. Incidentally,
within weeks of our broken relationship, Matt became
aware that his action had separated him from God and
he turned back to the Lord.

MEN OF HONOR

Because we are told that "Jabez was more honorable than
his brothers," we know that Jabez would not do certain
significant things his brothers would do, things which
affected a man's honor. He kept his word. Perhaps he did
business more honestly. Thus we also know that if the
brothers of Jabez had not rejected him outright, they certainly put an emotional distance between themselves and
him. Jesus tells us:

And this is the condemnation, that the light has come into the world, and men loved darkness rather than light, because their deeds were evil. (John 3:19)

When Jabez chose honor he risked rejection. Jesus exhibited ultimate honor. Wicked men tempted him; Jesus could have denied he was the Son of God and have avoided the cross. Yet Jesus valued truth above all suffering. He was Honor, He is Truth.

If you decide to follow Jabez to healing and to God or if you are already following God, be prepared for rejection. A holy, honorable, pure and loving life is certain to offend some and cause you to suffer the pain of rejection.

MEN OF LOVE

From their lives of honor, pain, rejection, prayer and desire to be a blessing emerges the very heart of God—a redemptive attitude toward pain: Love. I do not write just of feeling or philosophy when I speak of this type of love, rather this love puts others ahead of self.

For Jabez this love appears in his prayer that he not cause pain to others. Likewise, Jesus prayed upon the cross concerning those who had put him there, which I believe includes you and me, "Father, forgive them, for they do not know what they do" (Luke 23:34). This theme of God turning pain into redemptive love starts with the first promise of the Messiah, called in Genesis 3:15 "her seed"—the seed of woman. The Genesis promise is that the Seed, the Messiah, would be wounded but would destroy the tempter, the serpent:

And I will put enmity between you [the serpent] and the woman, and between your seed and her seed; He shall bruise your head, and you shall bruise His heel. (Genesis 3:15)

Out of Messiah's pain, deliverance for humanity would emerge. Suffering would bring redemption. The decision not to turn pain into bitterness, hatred or vengeance but instead into forgiveness and healing is the characteristic of the God of Israel and his Messiah Jesus.

"... who for the joy that was set before Him endured the cross ... " (Hebrews 12:2)

The ultimate healing then, transcends the removal or absence of pain. To be fully healed is to understand and embrace pain as an opportunity to change by becoming more like God. It means to take our pain and find a way to use it for good. The hurts in our hearts and bodies may cease, or they may linger. Nevertheless as they are healed they will feel different. Our pain becomes worthwhile, bearable, as it has purpose.

The apostle Paul ties pain and closeness to Jesus together in his heart cry: "That I might know the fellowship of his suffering and the power of his resurrection" (*see* Philippians 3:10). Paul understood he would to grow closer to God by sharing, with the right attitude, in the suffering which Jesus experienced.

Dearest Reader, please understand that if your heart is seeking God then the pain you feel is a loving warning to keep you from some greater harm to yourself or others. It is an opportunity to come closer to Jesus or it is a signpost pointing to healing and deeper significance for your life. Your pain may bring all three of these blessings. Yes, pain results from sin, our sin, sin against us and inherited sin. Yet pain can be a path to God and Godly love if you will choose it. God wants to relieve and heal your pain. He also wants to transform it from curse into blessing, a wonderful sorrow that leaves no regrets.

MEN OF FORGIVENESS

Jabez broke through his pain and the curse of his name by refusing to focus on those who hurt him and instead choosing to seek God's blessing. Have not we all known people who have ruined their lives by refusing to forgive and becoming bitter? In my opinion, Jabez's success from God would not have occurred unless and until he decided to have a loving and forgiving attitude toward his mother, brothers and, to the extent he was an influence, toward his father.

Jesus broke the cycle of sin when from the cross he forgave his crucifiers.

"Father forgive them for they do not know what they do."
(Luke 23:34)

As we have prayed with others for their healing, my wife Rosemary and I have seen powerful miracle restorations of body and of spirit when the sick person forgave those who had hurt him or her.

MEN OF EXPRESSIVE FAITH

At one time in my spiritual journey I felt that outward expression of my beliefs was not right. Partly I was afraid of the pain of disapproval by others. Partly, I guess, I bought into the politically correct canard that faith was purely personal, an interior experience to be kept to oneself. However, that phase was short lived. When I prayed that God would fill me with His Holy Spirit, I got a jolt of Acts Chapter 2! He routed my fear.

Consider that both Jabez and Jesus lived an expressive faith. With Jabez we know that he became known and was remembered for his prayer. The prayer of Jabez was not "silent asking." He cried out! In Jesus, all four Gospel writers show us a man who outwardly and dramatically expressed his faith in teaching, in healing, in prayer; at weddings, funerals and dinner parties. He used words, gestures and body language. When he refused to answer, he spoke loudest.

Both Jabez and Jesus were men of expressive faith. Expression leads to confidence. When love impels us to declare God's truth, it encourages and strengthens our own faith and the faith of those around us. "Faith comes through hearing the message of Messiah." (*see* Romans 10:17). We become confident. Jesus and Jabez were men of confident faith as well as expressive faith.

MEN OF CONFIDENT FAITH

The Apostle Paul wrote "I can do all things through Messiah who strengthens me" (*see* Philippians 4:13). This boast would be arrogant if it was not centered on Jesus. However, because it declares dependence on God, it exudes the confidence shown by both Jabez and Jesus.

Jabez cried out in prayer to God. We are not told whether his faith was small or hugely confident at that point. It seems to me that his "crying out" was more consistent with desperation than faith. If so can we still rightly see Jabez as a man of confident faith? Let me show you how.

The Bible explains that faith differs from belief. Whereas "belief" is mental acceptance of an idea, faith is belief plus the willingness to trust, rely and act upon the belief. Thus the common translation of John 3:16: "For God so loved the world that He gave His only begotten son that whosoever would *believe* in him would not perish but have eternal life," somewhat understates the demands upon the person who is called to "believe." Please permit me to paraphrase a fuller sense of John 3:16 based upon the context of all of the Bible:

> *For God so loved the world that He gave His only begotten son that whosoever would listen to, follow, trust, obey and love him would not perish but have eternal life.*

Faith is acting upon our belief. Did Jabez have faith, belief in action? When he prayed for enlarged territory almost certainly he had to act in accordance with a belief that God would answer. When I first started practicing law in the early 1970s, I conceived that the then current real estate boom in Chicago of converting high-rise apartment buildings from rental properties to condominiums could be extended to low rise, two- and three-story "walk-up" apartments. At one point Rosemary and

I identified a ten–unit rental building at 823–825 W. Oakdale as a particularly good candidate for conversion to condominium. I remember sitting in our car outside the building praying that God would allow us to buy that building. However, when it came on the market about a year later, we did not just call the owner and ask her to send the deed! Rather, I drafted a contract offer and we scrambled to find investors and financing. God allowed us to move from believing he would answer our prayer to a partnership faith that not only helped us get the building but successfully convert it to condominiums.

Likewise, as Jabez had his prayer for enlarged territory answered, it is unlikely that God simply had a deed delivered to his doorstep. God loves us too much to make us passive plastic stick figures in the real stuff of life. Jabez may have searched and bargained hard for enlarged territory. I certainly believe God allowed him to be a partner in obtaining his great blessing in life. Jabez acquired the blessing he prayed for because he participated with God in confident faith.

With Jesus, examples of confident faith abound. Consider three. At the beginning of his ministry Satan set before Jesus " … all the kingdoms of the world and their splendor" (Matthew 4:8 NIV), if only Jesus would worship him. Rejecting an offer which many would grab, Jesus replied: "It is written, worship the Lord your God and serve him only" (Matthew 4:10 NIV). As his crucifixion loomed, the Gospel of Luke tells us "he [Jesus] steadfastly set his face to Jerusalem" (Luke 9:51). And as we have already noted, on the eve of his execution, Jesus decided "… Nevertheless, not my will but yours be done" (Luke 22:42). Even when confidence was hard to come by, Jesus trusted in the character and love of his Father above.

The faith of Jabez, the faith of Jesus, confident, determined belief in action, broke through to victory, a victory God wants *you* to celebrate!

MEN TRIUMPHANT

What became of Jabez's decision to turn from pain to healing? He prayed "… that You would keep me from evil, that I might not cause pain." The Bible says, "God granted his request"(*see* 1 Chronicles 4:10). His own pain was transformed into a heart to bless others. He stopped causing pain to others and became a healer. His territory was enlarged. He prospered. We have already seen how Jabez overcame the pain of his name.

We have also noted that the town which may have been named after him (1 Chronicles 2:55) became a center of learning, a place transmitting knowledge—probably knowledge of Torah, Israel's law. Jabez may have, in effect, founded what today we would call a "college town" where he could support and subsidize these scribes in their precious work. If so, a broken man, in his humility and dependence on God blessed countless others out of his pain. Further, the legacy of Jabez is healing right now through the pages of Scripture, the Word of God. Could it be that one of the very scribes (on a Jabez scholarship!) recording or recopying the genealogies of Israel, at the town of Jabez and under the inspiration of God's Spirit, inserted the story of Jabez, a blessing for you 2,500 years later?

The Scriptures, both those of Messianic anticipation and of Messianic fulfillment, clearly describe the results of the suffering of Messiah:

Yet it pleased the Lord to bruise Him; He has put Him to grief. When You [the Almighty] make His soul an offering for sin, He shall see His seed, He shall prolong His days, and the pleasure of the Lord shall prosper in His hand. He shall see the labor of His soul, and be satisfied. By His knowledge My righteous Servant shall justify many, For He shall bear their iniquities. (Isaiah 53:10–11)

But we see Jesus, who was made a little lower than the angels, for the suffering of death crowned with glory and honor, that He, by the grace of God, might taste death for everyone. For it was fitting for Him, for whom are all things and by whom are all things, in bringing many sons to glory, to make the captain of their salvation perfect through sufferings. (Hebrews 2:9–10)

… He learned obedience by the things which He suffered. And having been perfected, He became the author of eternal salvation to all who obey Him, … (Hebrews 5:8–9)

Both Jabez and Jesus, though on vastly different levels, saw breakthroughs resulting from their redemptive hearts toward suffering. If your heart is willing to accept that all your pain had a good purpose, a *redemptive* purpose, then God has a breakthrough for you!

6

YOU CAN BE LIKE THEM

Let us recount the parallels between Jabez and Jesus:

> Men of Judah;
> Source of Pain;
> Men of Sorrows;
> Men of Prayer;
> Haters of Pain;
> Men of Honor;
> Men of Love;
> Men of Forgiveness;
> Men of Expressive Faith;
> Men of Confident Faith;
> Men Triumphant.

We learn from their lives that pain can be changed into blessing. If we want that blessing, let us adopt their attitude of heart and prayer. Let us apply the Jabez/Jesus parallels to ourselves. We cannot all become men of Judah, but we can all, by faith, become children of their forefather, Abraham. The next step is not too hard: most of us have already been a source of pain to our mothers! Nevertheless we can all impart healing pain, tough love to others. As to Godly sorrow, prayer, hating of pain, honor, love, forgiveness, expressive and confident faith and triumph, they are all station stops on the journey of faith. We need to board the train!

For the follower of Jesus, the Bible has this promise:

The Spirit Himself bears witness with our spirit that we are children of God, and if children, then heirs of God and joint heirs with Messiah, if indeed we suffer with Him, that we may also be glorified together. (*see* Romans 8:16–17)

Here is an honest prayer for a follower of Jesus:

"Father, I come to you in Jesus' name. You know my pain inside and how I hurt. Help me to see truly the ways I may have caused this pain and how I need to repent. Help me also, to let go of the anger and bitterness it has caused me. In fact, Father, I release that anger and bitterness now. Lord, others have a part in bringing this pain upon me. Give them the grace to see the evil they have done and to repent as I have now decided not to hate or hold bitterness against them. I will forgive them whenever they ask. Let me be like Jabez. Let me be like Jesus.

Jesus, the Bible says you are the same, yesterday, today and forever. It also says you healed all who came to you. Heal this wounded heart of mine. Heal my body also. I now receive that healing. I also now decide to turn my pain into a source of blessing for myself and others through the pain you are healing me of. Help me to see and take every opportunity you give me to bless others. Thank You. Amen."

Now, Christian sister or brother, you need to cooperate with this prayer as Jabez cooperated with his prayer. Keep praying it daily until you have assurance in your heart that you mean it fully. Now you are ready to do the works that will bring your suffering into the fullness of healing that God wants for you *and* those around you. Listen to how God instructed Israel in their religious duty and apply this instruction to your own healing process:

Is this not the fast that I have chosen: to loose the bonds of wickedness, to undo the heavy burdens, to let the oppressed go free, and that you break every yoke? Is it not to share your bread with the hungry, and that you bring to your house the poor who are cast out; When you see the naked, that you cover him, and not hide yourself from your own flesh?

Then your light shall break forth like the morning, your healing shall spring forth speedily, and your righteousness shall go before you; the glory of the Lord shall be your rear guard! Then you shall call, and the Lord will answer. (Isaiah 58:6–9a) (Emphasis added)

Reader, if you are not yet a follower of Jesus you can open your heart to follow, you can embrace, the man to whom the life of Jabez and all the prophets point. This man is the man of sorrows, the suffering servant of Isaiah 53. He is "the Lamb of God who takes away the sin of the World" hailed in John 1:29. He is Jesus. Not only will you find healing and purpose in the pain you have suffered, you will find freedom, friends and the path to eternal life. You will also find the pain of persecution:

So Jesus answered and said "Assuredly, I say to you, there is no one who has left house or brothers or sisters or father or mother or wife or children or lands, for my sake and the gospel's, who shall not receive a hundredfold now in this time—houses and brothers and sisters and mother and children and land, with persecutions—and in the age to come, eternal life. (Mark 10:29–30) (Emphasis supplied)

Here is a prayer to start you on the journey with Jesus:

"O God of Jabez, God of Israel, God of all creation, and God of Jesus, I have put myself, my pain, my needs, my ambitions and wants instead of You at the center of my life. I was wrong. I have hurt others and hurt myself, this was wrong. I have not accepted the forgiveness you have offered me by sending your son, the Messiah Jesus to die as a substitute for my sins. This too was wrong.

I now turn away from these wrongs and set my heart and will to follow you. Most of all I accept the love and forgiveness you offer me in Jesus. I now accept that he died for me on the cross and that he rose from the dead assuring me death was defeated and opening for me the path to eternal life.

Jesus, you are now welcome in my heart and life. I give my will, my body, my pain, my needs, my possessions, my relationships, my future, and myself to you completely.

Thank You for saving me. Amen."

Did you pray this prayer sincerely? If so, you are now at peace with God and are on the road to eternal life with the assurance that Jesus himself will be on the road with you to guide and help you, even to carry you when the way grows too steep. Now you can turn to the preceding prayer for believers in Jesus and let Him heal your pain and turn it into blessing for you, others and the Lord himself. Jabez became like Jesus. Now it's your turn. You can become like Jesus!

Zechariah 12:10–13:6 (NIV)

"And I will pour out on the house of David and the inhabitants of Jerusalem a spirit of grace and supplication. They will look on me, the one they have pierced, and they will mourn for him as one mourns for an only child, and grieve bitterly for him as one grieves for a firstborn son … .

"On that day a fountain will be opened to the house of David and the inhabitants of Jerusalem, to cleanse them from sin and impurity … .

"On that day every prophet will be ashamed of his prophetic vision … . If someone asks him, 'What are these wounds on your body?' he will answer, 'The wounds I was given at the house of my friends.'

ABOUT THE AUTHOR

John W. Mauck is an attorney, speaker and biblical scholar who partners with men and women to discover God's powerful solutions amidst the pain of church splits, litigation and reconciliation counseling. The most satisfying moments in his thirty-year career as principal attorney of Mauck & Baker, LLC have occurred when his work resulted in churches being given the right to build, thus allowing the Gospel to be preached and lived. For John, "being a lawyer is about serving God."

In 2001, John wrote *Paul on Trial, the Book of Acts as a Defense of Christianity*, which received widespread academic acclaim, sold over 15,000 copies and was a finalist for the Evangelical Book of the Year. He has hosted a weekly Bible study for lawyers for thirty years. Discipleship is an integral part of John's life, and he has mentored over twenty-five people, helping them mature as followers of Jesus.

John received his B.A. from Yale University and his Juris Doctor from the University of Chicago Law School. He and his wife of thirty-five years, Rosemary, have four adult children and have been active in prayer and healing ministries at First Presbyterian Church of Evanston since 1983.

www.thehealingofjabez.com